SOME CALL IT
SCIENCE

*the*religion *of*evolution

HENRY M. MORRIS

D0594685

INSTITUTE
for CREATION
RESEARCH

Dallas, Texas
www.icr.org

SOME CALL IT SCIENCE

by Henry M. Morris, Ph.D.

First printing: September 2006
Second printing, revised: October 2008

ISBN: 0-932766-87-0

Please visit our website for other books and resources: www.icr.org.

Printed in the United States of America.

Back cover citation: Michael Ruse, "Saving Darwinism from the Darwinians," *National Post,* May 13, 2000, B-3.

CONTENTS

3

FOREWORD

When a person dies, his last will and testament is made public. Our father, Dr. Henry Morris, recently passed into glory and left this booklet as his final testimony. His life had been lived writing books and giving oral testimony to the superiority of the creation view of origins over the evolution view. He championed the Word of God, teaching its truthfulness and upholding its veracity. And now he is in the presence of his Creator/Savior, having all his remaining questions answered.

In life he was a brilliant man. Some suspect he was a speed reader with a photographic memory, traits which undergirded his scores of thoughtful books on numerous subjects. More importantly, he was a man of great faith in the Bible, believing that its Author knows all things, is able to communicate clearly, and doesn't lie. Careful, believing study of that Word and the world He created will lead to a right understanding. Henry Morris's life was spent in fruitful endeavors, not willing to waste one moment or utter one idle word. And now he leaves his last testament.

This book was written in the last weeks of his life and completed on his deathbed, needing only final touches by those left behind. Its outline summarizes his life's message.

It starts with the error of evolutionary thinking. There is no true scientific evidence that macroevolution is taking place, has ever taken place, or could take place. It certainly can't explain the exquisite design we see in living things. To subscribe to evolution, one must *believe* in evolution. It is a faith without supporting evidence.

Next, the book deals with both the biblical and scientific truthfulness of creation. Creation's view of history makes sense of the present evidence. But ideas have consequences, and the ideas of evolution have had dire consequences. The destructive political and moral thought systems of our world are all built on an evolutionary foundation. Furthermore, evolution is the anti-Christian worldview, which stands in opposition to the Christian faith.

Conversely, creation thinking is wholesome and has spawned good fruit. In individual lives, nations, and in world settings, its beneficial impact can easily be documented. Most importantly, creation is the foundation for salvation, for the Creator has become the Redeemer. Soon He will bring the entire scope of history to a climax, and He will reign as King. Best of all, because of what He has done, we can be with Him for all eternity.

Thus begins the final testimony of a truly great soldier of the King. He has put down his pen, received the commendation "Well done, thou good and faithful servant," and beckons you to join him.

John D. Morris

President
Institute for Creation Research

Henry M. Morris III

Chief Executive Officer
Institute for Creation Research

SOME CALL IT SCIENCE

Charles Darwin was right about the present "war of nature." Everywhere there is a ceaseless struggle for survival, a constant competition for food and mates, a battle to the death that leaves only a few to propagate the next generation of each species. A product of nineteenth century English culture that still paid lip service to the Bible, Darwin began to wonder how this cruel, wasteful, and inefficient war of nature could be reconciled with the Christian concept of an all-powerful, all-loving Creator.

The Bible blames human sin, not God, for the horrors of our present fallen world: an interlude of disease, decline, disaster, and death between God's perfect creation and the final restoration of peace and harmony through Jesus. What the Bible calls evil, Darwin called good, claiming that "from the war of nature, from famine and death . . . the production of the higher animals [evolution], directly follows."[1] Euphemistically calling it "natural selection," Darwin turned the evil of struggle and death (conquered by Christ) into a substitute for God, touting it as a means to explain all appearance of design without a Designer. Far fewer Christians would compromise with evolution if they realized how totally antithetical it is to the gospel of Christ.

> Professing themselves to be wise, they became fools,
> and changed the glory of the uncorruptible God into an
> image made like to corruptible man, and to birds, and
> fourfooted beasts, and creeping things.[2]

For centuries, Western culture was dominated by belief in a personal and political paradise restored by Jesus' conquest of sin and death. During the past century, however, the gospel of new life in Christ has been replaced by the Darwinian "gospel of death," the belief that millions of years of struggle and death has changed pond scum into people and that evolutionary progress will continue inexorably toward heaven on earth. When asked about Darwinism's chief

---

1. Charles Darwin, *The Origin of Species by Means of Natural Selection* (Philadelphia: David McKay, 1905), 474.
2. Romans 1:22–23.

impact on culture, Michael Denton, author of the pivotal *Evolution: A Theory in Crisis*, replied that it was "to make atheism possible, or at least respectable."[3]

Many for thousands of years had promoted progress through what Darwin named the "preservation of favored races in the struggle for life,"[4] and many more had tried to explain life and to build their lives without God. But Christianity at the time of the Roman Empire was dynamic and had quickly spread around the world. How could the Christian gospel of life lose its influence to another gospel, the evolutionary gospel of death? The answer is found in changing perceptions of reality, most particularly the nature and significance of science.

Unlike the religions and philosophies of man, the Christian faith is rooted in reality—the words and acts of the eternal I AM, the Lord God, maker of time, matter, energy, and space. Yet to explain the ultimately profound spiritual truth of the new birth to the Jewish scholar and leader Nicodemus, Jesus asked, "If I have told you earthly things, and ye believe not, how shall ye believe, if I tell you of heavenly things?"[5] Science is the systematic study of earthly things, the search for explanations of processes and patterns of order that can be tested objectively by verifiable observations in the real world. Science is based on the twin assumptions that the universe is ordered and that its order is comprehensible to the human mind. Both these assumptions are guaranteed by God's Word, and it is no accident that biblical faith gave birth to modern experimental science. The founders of many scientific disciplines saw God's Word reflected in God's world: both the ingenuity and elegance of God's design and man's opportunity, through applied science, to share in Christ's restoring ministry, setting right those things gone wrong in a corrupted creation.

Evolution reversed everything. Struggle and death became the solution, not the problem. After millions of years of struggle and death

---

3. Thomas Kelly, producer, "Puzzle of the Ancient Wing," *Man Alive* television series (Canadian Broadcasting Corporation, 1981).
4. Darwin, *The Origin of Species,* title page.
5. John 3:12.

produced people capable of abstract thought and utopian dreams, man created "god" in his image. Eve's subjection of God's Word to her opinion and her interpretations of limited evidence became the highest level of intellectual sophistication and rational morality, not sin. Additionally, evolutionists tried to turn science against the Bible that gave science its birth, and demeaned and demoted science from a search for truth about nature to a search for naturalistic explanations, i.e., a naturalistic religion that relativizes truth, deifies human opinion, and promotes atheistic humanism. Those politically incorrect who challenge the pandemic claim that science proves evolution and discredits the Bible are held up to public ridicule as ignorant anachronisms whose sub-scientific ramblings ought to be banned from the public square and certainly the public school classroom.

But is it science that supports evolution and disproves the Bible or is it "science falsely so called"?[6] Is evolution really based on scientific evidence and scientific procedures, or is it merely atheistic humanism dressed up in a lab coat to pirate scientific respectability? Are Christians being seduced by "another gospel"?[7] Because of their "itching ears,"[8] are Christians being led astray by false teachers? Are we facing the gnostic deification of human opinion about which Paul warned Timothy?

> O Timothy, keep that which is committed to thy trust, avoiding profane and vain babblings, and oppositions of science falsely so called: Which some professing have erred concerning the faith.[9]

One of the most amazing phenomena of these latter days is the successful promotion of evolutionism as the scientific worldview, when it is utterly devoid of any scientific proof or even any valid evidence. It is actually a religion of naturalism, or even atheism, pretending to be hard scientific fact. It dominates the teaching philosophy in all public schools and state colleges, and has even capti-

---

6. 1 Timothy 6:20.
7. 2 Corinthians 11:4.
8. 2 Timothy 4:3.
9. 1 Timothy 6:20–21.

vated the judicial system. But it is utterly false, useless, and harmful in society.

Evolution has paraded as a fact which everyone must believe, but when we become so injudicious as to ask for evidence, the evidence quickly seems to disappear. It is no wonder that evolutionists are anxious to suppress evidence and to censor any scientific criticism of evolution or discussion of alternate views.

THE VANISHING CASE FOR EVOLUTION

After a quarter century of losing scientific debates to creation scientists, evolutionary scientists are now sharing the defense of evolution with lawyers, judges, educators, the media, politicians, anti-Christian pressure groups, and even the clergy. Yet, even as the theory of evolution continues to increase its cultural influence, scientists in multiple disciplines increasingly point out the scientific shortcomings of evolution. All the following quotations are from highly qualified spokesmen who (unless otherwise noted) are fully committed to belief in evolution in spite of the problems they acknowledge, and, regardless of date, their comments are consistent with current thinking among evolutionists.

No Evolution at Present

The lack of a case for evolution is most clearly recognized by the fact that no one has ever seen evolution happen.

> Evolution, at least in the sense that Darwin speaks of it, cannot be detected within the lifetime of a single observer.[10]

Horizontal variations (e.g., the different variations of dogs) are not true evolution, of course, nor are mutations, which are always either neutral or harmful as far as all known mutations are concerned. A process which has never been observed to occur, in all human history, should not be called scientific.

Astonishingly, science's own journals contain no

---

10. David Kitts, "Paleontology and Evolutionary Theory," *Evolution* 28 (September 24, 1974): 466.

explanations. Since science is found in science journals and Darwinian explanations are absent, Darwinism is not science.[11]

No New Species

Charles Darwin is popularly supposed to have solved the problem of the origin of species in his famous 1859 book of that title. However, Harvard biologist Ernst Mayr, considered the nation's top evolutionist until he died, observed:

> Darwin never really did discuss the origin of species in his *On the Origin of Species.* [12]

Not only could Darwin not cite a single example of a new species originating, but neither has anyone else in the entire subsequent century of evolutionary study.

> No one has ever produced a species by mechanisms of natural selection. No one has gotten near it.[13]

> The formation of species has long represented one of the most central, yet also one of the most elusive, subjects in evolutionary biology. [14]

> Speciation remains a major problem.[15]

No Known Mechanism of Evolution

It is also a very curious fact that no one understands how evolution works. Evolutionists commonly protest that they know evolu-

11. Michael Behe, "Denying Darwin: David Berlinski and Critics," *Commentary*, (September 1996): 22.
12. Niles Eldredge, *Time Frames: The Rethinking of Darwinian Evolution and the Theory of Punctuated Equilibria* (New York: Simon and Schuster, 1985), 33. Eldredge cites Mayr from his book *Systematics and the Origin of Species* (1942).
13. Colin Patterson, "Cladistics," Interview on BBC (March 4, 1982). Dr. Patterson was the senior paleontologist at the British Museum of Natural History.
14. S. R. Palumbi, "Marine Speciation," *Annual Review of Ecology and Systematics* (1994): 548.
15. Trevor Palmer, *Controversy—Catastrophism and Evolution: The Ongoing Debate* (Norwell, MA: Kluwer Academic, 1999), 322.

tion is true, but they cannot seem to determine its mechanism.

> Evolution is...troubled from within by the troubling complexities of genetic and developmental mechanisms and new questions about the central mystery—speciation itself.[16]

One would think that in the over 150 years following Darwin, with thousands of trained biologists studying the problem and using millions of dollars worth of complex lab equipment, they would have worked it out by now; but the mechanism which originates new species is still the "central mystery."

> Little evidence about the possible mechanism of evolution has been provided by the fossil record, so attention has focused on studies involving living organisms. Without any significant dimension of time, these have been able to give no more than hints as to how new species may arise under natural conditions. [17]

Even to the believing eye of the evolutionist beholder, the real world study of both fossils and extant organisms provides "no more than hints" about any hypothesized evolutionary mechanisms.

No Fossil Evidence

It was formerly claimed that the best evidence for evolution was the fossil record, but the fact is that billions of known fossils have not yet yielded a single unequivocal transitional series with transitional structures in the process of evolving.

> The known fossil record fails to document a single example of phyletic evolution accomplishing a major morphologic transition.[18]

This ubiquitous absence of intermediate forms is true not only for "major morphologic transitions" but even for most species.

---

16. Keith S. Thompson, "The Meanings of Evolution," *American Scientist* 70 (September/October 1982): 529.
17. Palmer, *Controversy—Catastrophism and Evolution*, 121.
18. Steven M. Stanley, *Macroevolution: Pattern and Process* (San Francisco: W.M. Freeman and Co., 1979), 39.

As is now well known, most fossil species appear instantaneously in the fossil record, persist for some millions of years virtually unchanged, only to disappear abruptly.[19]

As Darwin noted in *Origin of Species*, the abrupt emergence of arthropods in the fossil record during the Cambrian presents a problem for evolutionary biology. There are no obvious simpler or intermediate forms—either living or in the fossil record—that show convincingly how modern arthropods evolved from worm-like ancestors. Consequently there has been a wealth of speculation and contention about relationships between the arthropod lineages. [20]

Simpler and intermediate forms are absent among both fossils and living species, so "contention about relationships" in the largest animal phylum must be based on a "wealth of speculation." The lack of scientific support for evolutionary speculation is particularly glaring in the case of primate fossils.

However, there are not enough fossil records to answer when, where, and how *H. sapiens* emerged.[21]

Fossil evidence of human evolutionary history is fragmentary and open to various interpretations. Fossil evidence of chimpanzee evolution is absent altogether.[22]

The trouble is we probably know more about the evolution of extinct trilobites than we do about human

---

19. Tom Kemp, "A Fresh Look at the Fossil Record," *New Scientist* 108 (December 5, 1985): 67. Dr. Kemp was curator of the University Museum at Oxford University.

20. Daniel Osorio, John Bacon, Paul Whitington, "The Evolution of Arthropod Nervous Systems," *American Scientist* 85 (May/June 1997): 244.

21. N. Takahata, "A Genetic Perspective on the Origin and History of Humans," *Annual Review of Ecology and Systematics* 26 (1995): 355.

22. Henry Gee, "Palaeontology: Return to the Planet of the Apes," *Nature* 412 (July 2001):131.

evolution.[23]

As a result, many modern evolutionists, especially paleoanthropologists, agree with the following assessment:

In any case, no real evolutionist...uses the fossil record as evidence in favor of the theory of evolution as opposed to special creation.[24]

No Order in the Fossils

Not only are there no true transitional forms in the fossils, there is not even any general evidence of evolutionary progression in the actual fossil sequences.

The fossil record of evolution is amenable to a wide variety of models ranging from completely deterministic to completely stochastic. [25]

I regard the failure to find a clear "vector of progress" in life's history as the most puzzling fact of the fossil record....We have sought to impose a pattern that we hoped to find on a world that does not really display it.[26]

One of the most difficult problems in evolutionary paleontology has been the almost abrupt appearance of the major animal groups—classes and phyla—in full-fledged form, in the Cambrian and Ordovician periods. This must reflect a sudden acquisition of skeletons by

23. Douglas Palmer, "One Great Leap for Mankind," *New Scientist* 173 [2334] (March 16, 2002): 50.
24. Mark Ridley, "Who Doubts Evolution?" *New Scientist* 90 [1259] (June 25, 1981): 831. Dr. Ridley was Professor of Zoology at Oxford University when this statement was written.
25. David M. Raup, "Probabilistic Models in Evolutionary Biology," *American Scientist* 166 (January/February 1977): 57.
26. Stephen J. Gould, "The Ediacaran Experiment," *Natural History* 93 (February 1984): 23. Dr. Gould, Professor of Geology at Harvard, was arguably the nation's most prominent modern evolutionist until his death in 2002.

the various groups, in itself a problem.[27]

The superficial appearance of an evolutionary pattern in the fossil record has actually been imposed on it by the fact that the rocks containing the fossils have themselves been dated by their fossils.

> And this poses something of a problem: If we date the rocks by their fossils, how can we then turn around and talk about patterns of evolutionary change through time in the fossil record?[28]

> A circular argument arises: Interpret the fossil record in the terms of a particular theory of evolution, inspect the interpretation, and note that it confirms the theory. Well, it would, wouldn't it?[29]

The circularity of the evolutionist's argument and the imposition of Darwinian belief on fossils that show no such pattern starkly expose the pseudo-scientific nature of evolutionary thinking. Scientists searching the paleontological data for patterns of order would never come to the conclusion that chance mutations guided by millions of years of struggle and death gradually and progressively converted simple life into a myriad of increasingly complex and varied forms. Science has opposed that view from its inception.

Even as Darwin was giving birth to evolutionary theory, he admitted his view was completely contradicted by the fossil evidence.

> Why then is not every geological formation and every stratum full of such intermediate links? Geology assuredly does not reveal any such finely graduated organic chain; and this, perhaps, is the most obvious and serious objection which can be urged against the theory.[30]

Darwin tried to blame the conflict between his theory and the

---

27. Alfred G. Fisher, "Fossil record," in *Grolier Multimedia Encyclopedia* 2002 (i3) [CD-ROM]. See also Stephen J. Gould, "The Return of the Hopeful Monster." *Natural History* 86 (June/July 1977): 22-30.
28. Eldredge, *Time Frames*, 52.
29. Kemp, "A Fresh Look," 66.
30. Darwin, *Origin*, 293–94.

fossil facts on the imperfection of the geologic record. But 150 years of excavating thousands of tons of fossils have only confirmed Darwin's worst fears: Fossils are "the most obvious and serious objection" to evolutionary theory.

Paleontologists have actually discovered patterns of order among fossils which expose the errors of evolution and offer scientific support to the scriptural account of earth's history. The sudden appearance of abundant life forms, complete and complex, in the lowest fossil-rich layer (the so-called Cambrian explosion) suggests prior acts of special creation. The fossil record of death, decline, and disaster is consistent with the corruption of creation by man's sin and the colossal catastrophe of Noah's Flood. The association of fossils with evolution in the public mind (and the public school classroom) is a triumph of salesmanship, not science. True science, the study of God's world, points instead to the truth of God's Word. Yet, while scientific truth supports scriptural truth, too many Christians are still seduced by the slick sales pitch of "science falsely so called," and as Paul warned, they "have erred concerning the faith."[31]

No Evidence that Evolution Is Possible

The basic reason that there is no scientific evidence of evolution in the present or the past is that the law of increasing entropy, or the second law of thermodynamics, contradicts the very premise of evolution. The evolutionist assumes that the whole universe has evolved upward from a single primeval particle to human beings, but the second law (one of the best-proved laws of science) states that the whole universe is running down into complete disorder.

> How can the forces of biological development and the forces of physical degeneration be operating at cross purposes? It would take, of course, a far greater mind than mine even to attempt to penetrate this riddle.... I can only pose the question.[32]

Evolutionists often attempt to sidestep this question by assert-

---

31. 1 Timothy 6:21.
32. Sydney Harris, "Second Law of Thermodynamics," *San Francisco Examiner* (January 27, 1984).

ing that the second law applies only to isolated systems. But this is wrong!

> The quantity of entropy generated locally cannot be negative irrespective of whether the system is isolated or not.[33]

> Ordinarily the second law is stated for isolated systems, but the second law applies equally well to open systems.[34]

Entropy can be forced to decrease in an open system if enough organizing energy and information is applied to it from outside the system. The externally-introduced complexity would have to be adequate to overcome the normal internal increase in entropy when raw energy is added from outside. However, no such external source of organized and energized information is available to the supposed evolutionary process. Raw solar energy is not organized information!

As too many people discover each summer, raw solar energy has a powerful disorganizing and destructive effect on human skin. Green plants can use that same solar energy to grow, but the credit goes not to the raw energy, but to the information and organization God built into the intricate molecular machinery of photosynthesis when He created green plants "pleasant to the sight, and good for food."[35]

No Evidence from Similarities

The existence of similarities between organisms—whether in external morphology or internal biochemistry—is easily explained as the Creator's design of similar systems for similar functions. However, such similarities are not explicable by common evolutionary descent.

It is now clear that the pride with which it was

---

33. Arnold Sommerfeld, *Thermodynamics and Statistical Mechanics* (New York: Academic Press, 1956), 155.
34. John Ross, Letter to the Editor, *Chemical and Engineering News* (July 7, 1980): 40. Ross was at Harvard University when this was written.
35. Genesis 2:9.

assumed that the inheritance of homologous structures from a common ancestor explained homology was misplaced.[36]

The really significant finding that comes to light from comparing the proteins' amino acid sequences is that it is impossible to arrange them in any sort of an evolutionary series.[37]

At the present time, biologists still have not developed a phylogenetic system of taxonomy [classification].[38]

The proper relationship between systematic practice and our understanding of evolution has long been debated.[39]

So now what? We have two bodies of evidence, each with seemingly impeccable credentials, that lead us to mutually contradictory conclusions—the same situation our predecessors faced at the end of the last century. If we believe the DNA, modern humans spread around the globe from Africa starting about 100,000 years ago. But if we accept that, we have to ignore evidence from the fossils, and if we believe the fossils, we have to ignore evidence from DNA.[40]

Both the origin of life and the origin of the major groups of animals remain unknown.[41]

Unable to find any evolutionary pattern of similarities on which to base the science of classification, evolutionists still use the pre-

---

36. Sir Gavin de Beer, *Homology, an Unsolved Problem* (London: Oxford University Press, 1971), 15. Sir Gavin was a leading European evolutionist.
37. Michael Denton, *Evolution: A Theory in Crisis* (London: Burnett Books, 1985), 289. Denton is a research microbiologist in Australia.
38. K. Queiroz and J. Gauthier, "Phylogenetic Taxonomy," *Annual Review of Ecology and Systematics* 23 (1992): 450.
39. David P. Mindell and Christine E. Thacker, "Rates of Molecular Evolution," *Annual Review of Ecology and Systematics* 27 (1996): 279.
40. James Trefil, *101 Things You Don't Know about Science and No One Else Does Either* (Boston: Houghton Mifflin, 1996), 268-69.
41. Fisher, "Fossil record," *Grolier Multimedia Encyclopedia.*

Darwinian taxonomic system developed by Carolus Linnaeus, the Christian man of science who founded systematics on the clear and explicit principles of Scripture.

No Recapitulation or Vestigial Organs

The old arguments for evolution based on the recapitulation theory (the idea that embryonic development in the womb reenacts the evolution of the species) and vestigial organs ("useless" organs believed to have been useful in an earlier stage of evolution) have long been discredited.

> [T]he theory of recapitulation...should be defunct today.[42]

> An analysis of the difficulties in unambiguously identifying functionless structures...leads to the conclusion that "vestigial organs" provide no evidence for evolutionary theory.[43]

> Long regarded as a vestigial organ with no function in the human body, the appendix is now thought to be one of the sites where immune responses are initiated.[44]

Ideas have consequences, and bad ideas have bad consequences. While it bowed to the idol of evolution, medical science ignored 180 structures in the human body decreed by Darwin and Haeckel to be useless leftovers of our evolutionary ancestry. Who knows how many healthy, disease-fighting tonsils and appendices were removed by evolutionary malpractice until medical science returned to its experimental basis and healing ministry and discovered the proper functions of these structures created with plan and purpose?

---

42. Stephen J. Gould, "Dr. Down's Syndrome," *Natural History* 89 (April 1980): 144.
43. S. R. Scadding, "Do 'Vestigial Organs' Provide Evidence for Evolution?" *Evolutionary Theory* 5 (May 1981): 173.
44. Roy Hartensteain, "Appendix," in *Grolier Multimedia Encycolpedia* 2001 (i3) [CD-ROM].

No Evidence from Molecular Biology

Evolutionists have been shocked into silence (or into shouting "separation of church and state") by DNA discoveries and the magnificent microminiaturized molecular machinery within living cells. Although they do not publicly tie creation with Christ, a burgeoning number of secular and agnostic scientists have joined creation scientists in the enthusiastic proclamation of the overwhelming biomolecular evidence of intelligent design.

> Domain shuffling aside, it remains a mystery how the undirected process of mutation, combined with natural selection, has resulted in the creation of thousands of new proteins with extraordinarily diverse and well-optimized functions. This problem is particularly acute for tightly integrated molecular systems that consist of many interacting parts, such as ligands, receptors, and the downstream regulatory factors with which they interact. In these systems it is not clear how a new function for any protein might be selected for unless the other members of the complex are already present, creating a molecular version of the ancient evolutionary riddle of the chicken and the egg.[45]

> There are no detailed Darwinian accounts for the evolution of any fundamental biochemical or cellular system, only a variety of wishful speculations.[46]

Faced with evidence from real science that supports creation, evolutionists are left with only "the ancient evolutionary riddle of the chicken and the egg" and "a variety of wishful speculations."

The Residual Case for Evolution

In spite of these admissions, all the scientists quoted above continued to believe in evolution. Each quotation noted is fully war-

---

45. Jospeh Thornton and Rob DeSalle, "Gene Family Evolution and Homology: Genomics Meets Phylogenetics," *Annual Review of Genomics and Human Genetics* 1 (2000): 64.
46. James Shapiro, "Darwin's Black Box: The Biochemical Challenge to Evolution" (Book Review), *National Review* (September 16, 1996).

ranted in context and could be further documented from other authorities also.[47]

What, then, remains of the case for evolution? Stephen Gould fell back on what he believed were "imperfections" in nature.

> If there were no imperfections, there would be no evidence to favor evolution by natural selection over creation.[48]

But this argument is essentially the same as the old discredited argument from vestigial organs and merely assumes man's present ignorance to be knowledge. Even if there are imperfections in nature (as well as harmful mutations, vestigial organs, extinctions, etc.), such trends are opposite to any imaginary evolutionary progress, so can hardly prove evolution.

There is one final argument, however. Gould's fellow atheist and Marxist at Harvard, geneticist Richard Lewontin, said:

> No one has ever found an organism that is known not to have parents, or a parent. This is the strongest evidence on behalf of evolution.[49]

That is, if one denies a Creator, the existence of life proves evolution! But apart from its necessity as a support for atheism or pantheism, there is clearly no scientific evidence for evolution, which is clearly no more than "science falsely so called."

The absence of evidence for evolution does not, by itself, prove creation, of course. Nevertheless, special creation is clearly the only alternative to evolution.

> Creation and evolution, between them, exhaust the possible explanations for the origin of living things. Organisms either appeared on the earth fully developed

---

47. See the many ICR books with such documentation (*The Modern Creation Trilogy, Scientific Creationism,* etc.).
48. As cited in Jeremy Cherfas, "The Difficulties of Darwinism," *New Scientist* 102 (May 17, 1984): 29.
49. As reported in an interview by Tom Bethell, "Agnostic Evolutionists: The Taxonimic Case Against Darwin," *Harper's* (February 1985): 61.

or they did not. If they did not, they must have developed from pre-existing species by some process of modification. If they did appear in a fully developed state, they must have been created by some omnipotent intelligence.[50]

While we admittedly cannot prove creation from science, it is important to note that all the above facts offered as evidence against evolution (gaps between kinds, no evolutionary mechanism, increasing entropy, etc.) are actual predictions from a creation model!

Creationists prefer the reasonable faith of creationism, which is supported by all the real scientific evidence, to the credulous faith of evolutionism, which is supported by no real scientific evidence. The question remains unanswered (scientifically, at least) as to why evolutionists prefer to believe in evolution.

THE STRONG FAITH OF THE EVOLUTIONIST

Christian faith is essential for salvation (Ephesians 2:8), but in one sense it is not all that difficult to have this kind of faith. After all, the amazing majesty, beauty, and complexity of the universe should make it easy to believe in a great Creator God;[51] and the overwhelming body of objective evidence for this historicity of the person and work of Jesus Christ—including His bodily resurrection from the grave—makes it easy enough to believe in His saving power.[52]

Illogical Faith

The faith of the evolutionist and humanist is of another order altogether. His is a splendid faith indeed, a faith not dependent on anything so mundane as evidence or logic, but rather a faith strong in its childlike trust, relying wholly on omniscient Chance and omnipotent Matter to produce the complex systems and mighty energies of the universe. The evolutionist's faith is not dependent on evidence, but is pure faith—absolute credulity.

---

50. D. J. Futuyma, *Science on Trial: The Case for Evolution* (New York: Pantheon Books, 1983), 197.
51. See Psalm 19:1 and Romans 1:20.
52. See the many evidences cited in Henry M. Morris's *Many Infallible Proofs*, (Green Forest, AR: Master Books, 1996), 9–106.

Harvard zoologist P. J. Darlington has penned a remarkable statement of this evolutionary faith in his book *Evolution for Naturalists*.
Acknowledging that the creative abilities of matter are entirely enig-
matic, he nevertheless bravely believes in them:

> The outstanding evolutionary mystery now is how
> matter has originated and evolved, why it has taken its
> present form in the universe and on the earth, and why
> it is capable of forming itself into complex living sets
> of molecules. This capability is inherent in matter as we
> know it, in its organization and energy.[53]

Is not this a fine statement of faith? Even after exploring many
avenues of potential evidence in his book, Professor Darlington,
more than 200 pages later, is still able to assert there is no evidence
and thus his faith is still pure.

> It is a fundamental evolutionary generalization that no
> external agent imposes life on matter. Matter takes the
> forms it does because it has the inherent capacity to do
> so....This is one of the most remarkable and mysterious
> facts about our universe: that matter exists that has the
> capacity to form itself into the most complex patterns
> of life.[54]

The evolutionist faces a great temptation here, a serious stumbling block to his faith. It seems utterly impossible that dead matter
could create life. At this point, surely, he will have to defer to logic
and acknowledge that life must be produced by a Cause which is
itself alive. After all, scientists long ago showed experimentally that
life comes only from life. Ah, but not so! The evolutionist's faith is
strong enough to surmount even this barrier.

> By this I do *not* mean to suggest the existence of a
> vital force or entelechy or universal intelligence, but
> just to state an attribute of matter as represented by the
> atoms and molecules we know....We do not solve the
> mystery by using our inadequate brains to invent mystic

---

53. P. J. Darlington, *Evolution for Naturalists* (New York: John Wiley, 1980), 15.
54. Ibid, 234.

explanations.[55]

Nor do we "solve the mystery" by using our "inadequate brains" to endow matter with properties contrary to those scientists actually observe. This faith in the life-generating powers of matter glows even more brightly in light of the confessed bafflement of those scientists most familiar with the nature of life and its inexplicable naturalistic origin. One of these has said:

> We do not understand even the general features of the origin of the genetic code....The origin of the genetic code is the most baffling aspect of the problem of the origins of life and a major conceptual or experimental breakthrough may be needed before we can make any substantial progress.[56]

In fact, the author of this confession, Dr. Orgel, seems at first to have wavered somewhat in his own faith. He and Dr. Francis Crick, a co-discoverer of the remarkably complex DNA molecule (now known to be a basic component of life and of the genetic code which controls the reproduction of all living systems), have acknowledged that life is too complex to have arisen naturalistically in the few billion years of earth history.

In actuality, however, their faith is still strong, perhaps even stronger than that of other evolutionists. They believe in "directed panspermia," the amazing notion that lifeseeds were planted on earth by an unknown civilization from some other world in outer space! The mere statement of this concept is itself adequate testimony to the grand credulity of the faith of these evolutionists, since there exists not one iota of scientific evidence for such ethereal civilizations and even less evidence that the properties of matter and laws of science that prevent chemical evolution on earth would be different somewhere else in space.

No Chance of a Creator

Another evolutionist of bold faith is Richard Dawkins, origina-

---

55. Ibid.
56. Leslie Orgel, "Darwinism at the Very Beginning of Life," *New Scientist* 94 (April 15, 1982): 151.

tor and popularizer of the remarkable concept of "selfish genes," an idea which itself bespeaks an unusual type of faith. Dawkins, who is on the zoology faculty at England's famed Oxford University, maintains an unshakeable faith in Darwinian evolution, even at the molecular level, in spite of all the modern attacks thereon by fellow evolutionists. He acknowledges, of course, that the logical thing is to believe in God.

> The more statistically improbable a thing is, the less can we believe that it just happened by blind chance. Superficially the obvious alternative to chance is an intelligent Designer.[57]

Even though it is, indeed, quite obvious that every complex and purposeful system which man has ever seen produced throughout history has been the product of an intelligent human designer, Professor Dawkins is willing to believe that life itself, far more complex that any man-made contrivance, was not designed. He dismisses God in these patronizing words:

> I am afraid I shall give God rather short shrift. He may have many virtues: no doubt he is invaluable as a pricker of the conscience and a comfort to the dying and bereaved, but as an explanation of organized complexity he simply will not do. It is organized complexity we are trying to explain, so it is footling to invoke in explanation a being sufficiently organized and complex to create it.[58]

He is right, of course. It requires only a very ordinary sort of faith to explain a given effect by a course adequate to produce the effect. Much more faith is required, an extraordinary faith, to believe that effects are produced by causes that are not able to produce them! To believe that non-living matter can create life, that chaotic disorder can evolve itself into organized complexity, that unthinking atoms can sort themselves into thinking human beings—here is

---

57. Richard Dawkins, "The Necessity of Darwinism," *New Scientist* 94 (April 15, 1982): 130.
58. Ibid.

a worthy faith!

Mixing Faith and Science

If faith must be excluded from the public science classroom, then evolution does not belong there. At least the creationist relates his faith to facts in the real world. Science imposes no constraints on the source of hypotheses but does demand that they be tested against repeatable, verifiable observations of reality. Creationists may derive hypotheses in part from biblical principles and history, but they test their scientific hypotheses about DNA, Grand Canyon, genetic variability, etc., against experimental evidence and real-world observations. Not so with evolution. Instead of basing evaluation of hypotheses on evidence, evolutionists base their hypotheses on hypotheses. In assessing the legacy of Darwinism for the centenary edition of Darwin's *Origin*, R. W. Thompson put it this way:

> Thus are engendered those fragile towers of hypotheses based on hypotheses, in which fact and fiction intermingle in inextricable confusion.[59]

Thanks to the force-feeding of evolution in our public school classrooms, students may suffer under the confusion of intermingling fact and fiction in evolutionary science.

Faith in Every Field

Evolutionary faith is not limited to biologists, of course. It can be appropriated by evolutionary humanists in philosophy, in economics, in politics, in all fields. A first-rate example was Adolph Hitler, whose implicit faith in Darwinism ("the preservation of favored races in the struggle for life," as the subtitle of Darwin's *Origin of Species* puts it) gave him the vision and courage to array his assumed master race against the world, believing that its triumph would be for the greater good of all mankind in its ongoing evolutionary progress. Although his armies finally went down to defeat, he still retained his great faith!

Hitler believed in struggle as a Darwinian principle of

---

59. W. R. Thompson, introduction to *Origin of Species* by Charles Darwin, (London: Dent/Everyman's Library, 1956).

human life that forced every people to try to dominate all others; without struggle they would rot and perish.... Even in his own defeat in April 1945 Hitler expressed his faith in the survival of the stronger and declared the Slavic peoples to have proven themselves the stronger.[60]

Note the strong and unselfish evolutionary faith of Adolph Hitler, willing even to sacrifice his entire Teutonic race and finally to take his own life, to advance the cause of evolution.

Finally, let us consider the remarkable faith of Isaac Asimov, the most prolific science writer of our age. Asimov believed that our present universe began with the big bang of a primeval cosmic egg, whose initial explosion led to the formation of chemical elements, stars, galaxies, and finally, people. Now note his fine statement of faith.

The cosmic egg may be structureless (as far as we know), but it apparently represented a very orderly conglomeration of matter. Its explosion represented a vast shift in the direction of disorder, and ever since, the amount of disorder in the Universe has been increasing.[61]

Explosions commonly produce disorder and disintegration, so this greatest of all explosions must have produced the ultimate in disorder and disintegration. Evolution requires, however, that the great bang somehow yield great order and complex structures. Dr. Asimov, therefore, believes that the primeval egg possessed an almost infinitely high degree of order, even though it had no structure.

Herein we encounter Asimov's deep faith. In all normal systems with which scientists work, *structure* and *order* are essentially synonymous, equivalent also to *information, complexity, organization, integration,* and other such terms. If it did what evolutionists believe it did, the primeval egg certainly must have possessed a tremendous amount of organizing information, and it thus seems nonsensical to

60. P. Hoffman, *Hitler's Personal Security: Protecting the Führer* (London: Pergamon, 1979), 264.
61. Isaac Asimov, *In the Beginning* (New York: Crown Publishers, 1981), 24.

say it had no structure. Asimov believed not only in run-of-the-mill impossibilities but in the equivalence of opposites (no structure = high order).

However, Dr. Asimov did feel it necessary to attempt some kind of rationalization, knowing that people of lesser faith might otherwise stumble.

> The existence of the cosmic egg is, however, itself something of an anomaly. If the general movement of the universe is from order to disorder, how did the order (which presumably existed in the cosmic egg) originate? Where did it come from?[62]

At this point, he makes another leap of faith, proposing that the universe—instead of expanding, as he believes it is doing now—was contracting, with everything somehow in reverse and with its order increasing as it contracted. For this to be possible, of course, gravitational attraction has to be invoked to pull it together. The problem with the belief, however, is that the total mass of the matter in the universe is far too small to allow this ever to happen. Worse, if gravitational collapse of the universe did occur, the random thermal energy generated would destroy any and all remaining structure, order, and information.

Such a problem as this could not overcome the faith of Asimov. He handled it merely by another act of faith.

> I have a hunch that the "missing mass" required to raise the density to the proper figure will yet be found and that the universe will yet be discovered to oscillate.[63]

Asimov's hunch, therefore, solves it all.

We creationists, admittedly, find it difficult to believe all these things that evolutionists manage to believe. But we have always had a high regard for the principle of faith, even though our own faith is rather weak, based as it is on such strong evidence as almost to compel belief in the God of creation and redemption. We must,

---

62. Ibid.
63. Ibid, 25.

therefore, at least express admiration for the remarkable faith of the evolutionist.

EVOLUTIONARY PANTHEISM

It has thus been shown, admittedly with a touch of sarcasm, that belief in evolution is not based on scientific fact, but on faith. I should apologize for the sarcasm, because many evolutionists are good men and women, capable laboratory scientists, and sometimes even professing Christians. But the truth is they have to believe in evolution. They cannot see it in action (variation within the kind is not evolution in the ultimate sense, although some may use the term *microevolution*). It is only macroevolution—the increase in complexity required to cause one kind to evolve into a different and higher kind—that is questioned. So evolutionists have to believe evolution happened in the past, despite the law of entropy and the lack of fossil evidence of any transitional series.

That faith seems to be pure naturalism or even atheism (since evolutionists will make no allowances for God or the supernatural anywhere in the process), but evolutionists often resent being viewed as atheists. Just what is their religion, then?

It seems in many cases to be a form of pantheism.

Ever since Darwin, the concept of natural selection has dominated evolutionary thought, providing a naturalistic explanation, at the expense of truth, for the origin of species and thus (as Julian Huxley used to say) eliminating the need for God. In recent years, however, there has been a strong reaction against Darwinian evolution in many places. Unfortunately, the change has not caused these scientists to return to creationism, but instead, to pre-Darwinian evolutionism. That is, they are abandoning atheistic evolution and returning to pantheistic evolution. In fact, this is the pseudo-scientific rationale underlying the so-called New Age movement which is sweeping over the world today.

Evolution in Antiquity

Evolutionism is not a modern scientific theory at all but is as old as human rebellion against the Creator.

In fact, the belief that life has its origins in a single basic substance is so widespread among the various peoples of the world, primitive or civilized, that it can be considered one of the few universal themes in the history of ideas.[64]

That "basic substance" out of which all things have evolved is usually said to have been the primeval watery chaos which had existed from eternity. From this evolved the gods and goddesses who produced everything else. This universal belief of antiquity is not just primitive mythology, of course.

But these deities are...actually personifications of Nature, and their activities, predictable and unpredictable, determine what life will be like on Earth.[65]

Dr. Stanley Jaki, with doctorates in both physics and theology and author of thirty-two books, confirms the universality of ancient pagan evolutionism:

All of these ancients were pagan. The essence of paganism, old and new, is that the universe is eternal, that its motives are without beginning and without end. Belief in creation out of nothing is the very opposite of paganism.[66]

As far as the post-Flood world is concerned, this pagan evolutionism originated in ancient Babylon, in the land of Sumer, but then spread around the world with the dispersion, as described in Genesis 11. It came to full flower in Greece, especially through the writings of Homer and Hesiod.

In biblical thought, the earth is not our mother; it is the home our Father gave us. In pagan evolutionism, however, the earth itself was considered to be the mother of all living things. The Greek goddess of the earth, Gaia (with equivalent names in other ethnic religions),

---

64. Ernest L. Abel, *Ancient Views on the Origin of Life* (Madison, NJ: Fairleigh Dickinson University Press, 1973), 15.
65. Ibid, 15.
66. Stanley L. Jaki, "Science: Western or What?" *Intercollegiate Review* 26 (Fall 1990): 8.

soon became recognized as Mother Earth or Mother Nature.

How did we reach our present secular humanist world? In times that are ancient by human measure, as far back as the earliest artifacts can be found, it seems that the Earth was worshipped as a goddess and believed to be alive. The myth of the great Mother is part of most early religions.[67]

Return to Gaia

The author cited above is a brilliant scientist and has been one of the leaders in developing the modern Gaian Hypothesis, which views the earth as an actual living organism, evolving itself while controlling the geological evolution of its crust and the biological evolution of its plants and animals.

The evolution of the species and the evolution of their environment are tightly coupled together as a single and inseparable process.[68]

Lovelock and other leading Gaians do not think of Gaia as a real woman living on Mount Olympus or somewhere—at least in effect—but as a living, intelligent being comprising the earth and all its evolving organisms and other systems.

Another distinguished scientist who has advocated evolutionary pantheism is Rupert Sheldrake, with a Ph.D. from Cambridge University and later director of studies in cell biology there.

But today, with the rise of the green movement, Mother Nature is reasserting herself, whether we like it or not. In particular, the acknowledgement that our planet is a living organism, Gaia, Mother Earth, strikes a responsive chord in millions of people.[69]

As Dr. Sheldrake indicates, the modern green movement, which

67. James Lovelock, *The Ages of Gaia* (New York: W. W. Norton and Co., 1988), 208.
68. Ibid, 12.
69. Rupert Sheldrake, *The Rebirth of Nature: The Greening of Science and God* (New York: Bantam Books, 1991), 10.

has rapidly grown all over the world, is largely committed to this concept of pantheistic evolution. In fact, the environmental activists in politics, both local and national, are strongly influenced by such ideas.

> Lovelock's musings have had two consequences. They inspired a quasi-political movement based in London, complete with a publishing arm, that now includes thousands of adherents throughout the U. S. and Western Europe. Indeed, Gaia has almost become the official ideology of "Green" parties in Europe: it appeals naturally to scientifically innocent individuals who worry about the environment.[70]

This theme is often emphasized in public school classrooms today. A recent vice president of the United States had a best-selling 1992 book, *Earth in the Balance: Ecology and the Human Spirit*, which passionately espouses such concepts.

The worship of Mother Earth is also becoming prominent in some aspects of the modern feminist movement. The more radical feminists, in fact, are replacing God with "The Goddess," even holding worship services in "her" name. In fact, former Vice President Al Gore, on page 260 of his book, cites with approval the statement that "the prevailing ideology of belief in prehistoric Europe and much of the world was based on the worship of a single earth goddess," lamenting the fact that "organized goddess worship was eliminated by Christianity."[71] Now "organized goddess worship" is trying to eliminate Christianity. Unfortunately, too many Christians cannot hear the battle trumpet sound over the din of compromise.

Cosmic Pantheism

In fact, the idea of pantheistic evolution is not even limited to that of earth and its systems. Modern New Age believers embrace the whole universe in some form of conscious cosmic evolution. The famous astronomer Fred Hoyle, in fact, wrote an entire book,

---

70. Tim Beardsley, "Gaia," *Scientific American* 261 (December 1989): 35.
71. Al Gore, *Earth in the Balance: Ecology and the Human Spirit* (New York: Plume, 1993), 260.

entitled *The Intelligent Universe,*[72] rejecting terrestrial Darwin-type evolution in favor of cosmic pantheistic evolution. Another British astronomer and physicist, Paul Davies, thinks that modern notions of order from chaos somehow prove that the "creative cosmos" has created itself.

> In recent years, more scientists have come to recognize that matter and energy possess an innate ability to self-organize.[73]

Citing no evidence to support his belief and ignoring evidence which contradicts it, he "proves" his point merely by boldly asserting it. He cites

> the astonishing ability of an embryo to develop from a single strand of DNA, via an exquisitely well-organized sequence of formative steps, into an exceedingly complex organism.[74]

Confident his trust in Mother Nature will go unquestioned, Dr. Davies makes no scientific attempt to explain just how the DNA self-programmed itself to do this. In any case, this is exactly what more and more scientists believe today. Sheldrake in fact has said:

> All nature is evolutionary. The cosmos is like a great developing organism, and evolutionary creativity is inherent in nature herself.[75]

But that is not all. Sheldrake goes on to state:

> The universe as a whole is a developing organism, and so are the galaxies, solar systems, and biospheres within it, including the earth.[76]

It is not possible in our limited space to discuss this further, but the fact is that there is no more scientific proof (or even real evi-

---

72. Fred Hoyle, *The Intelligent Universe* (London: Michael Joseph Co., 1983).
73. Paul Davies, "The Creative Cosmos," *New Scientist* 116 (December 17, 1987): 42.
74. Ibid.
75. Rupert Sheldrake, *Rebirth of Nature*, 95.
76. Ibid, 151.

dence) for pantheistic evolution than for atheistic evolution. Evolution in any form is nothing but "cunningly devised fables" and "science falsely so called."[77]

As the Catholic physicist Dr. Wolfgang Smith has said:

> The point, however, is that the doctrine of evolution has swept the world, not on the strength of its scientific merits, but precisely in its capacity as a Gnostic myth. It affirms, in effect, that living beings created themselves, which is, in essence, a metaphysical claim....Thus, in the final analysis, evolutionism is in truth a metaphysical doctrine decked out in scientific garb.[78]

The highly publicized book and movie on the alleged Da Vinci Code constitute a strong attempt to revive the gnostic philosophy, placing, as Eve did, men's words above God's Word. To establish the counterfeit faith of modern gnosticism, *The Da Vinci Code* must first discredit the real God, using Hollywood to sell fiction as fact and fact as fiction, counting on Christian compromisers to have dulled interest in and knowledge of biblical truth.

EVOLUTION AND THE NEW AGE

So a strange religion has thus been coming into prominence in recent years. Often mistakenly called the New Age movement, this phenomenon is in reality a complex of modern science and ancient paganism, featuring systems theory, computer science, and mathematical physics along with astrology, occultism, religious mysticism, and nature worship. Ostensibly offered as a reaction against the sterile materialism of Western thought, this influential system appeals both to man's religious nature and his intellectual pride. Its goal is to become the world's one religion.

Although New Age followers have a form of religion, their "god" is evolution, not the true God of creation. Many New Age followers regard the controversial priest Teilhard de Chardin as their spiritual

---

77. 2 Peter 1:16 and 1 Timothy 6:20.
78. Wolfgang Smith, *Teilhardism and the New Religion* (Rockford, IL: Tan Books and Publishers, 1988), 242.

father. His famous statement of faith was as follows:

> [Evolution] is a general postulate to which all theories, all hypotheses, all systems must henceforward bow and which they must satisfy in order to be thinkable and true. Evolution is a light which illuminates all facts, a trajectory which all lines of thought must follow.[79]

The ethnic religions of the East (Hinduism, Taoism, Buddhism, Confucianism, etc.) which in large measure continue the polytheistic pantheism of the ancient pagan religions, have long espoused evolutionary views of the universe and its living things and so merge naturally and easily into the evolutionary framework of the New Age philosophy. It is surprising, however, to find that Julian Huxley and Theodosius Dobzhansky, two of the most prominent of the western, scientific neo-Darwinians, were early proponents of this modern evolutionary religion. In a eulogy following Dobzhansky's death, geneticist Francisco Ayala said:

> Dobzhansky was a religious man, although he apparently rejected fundamental beliefs of traditional religion, such as the existence of a personal God.... Dobzhansky held that in man, biological evolution has transcended itself into the realm of self-awareness and culture. He believed that mankind would eventually evolve into higher levels of harmony and creativity. He was a metaphysical optimist.[80]

Dobzhansky himself penned the following typical New Age sentiment:

> In giving rise to man, the evolutionary process has, apparently for the first and only time in the history of the Cosmos, become conscious of itself.[81]

---

79. Franciso Ayala, "Nothing in Biology Makes Sense Except in the Light of Evolution: Theodosius Dobzhansky, 1900-1975," *Journal of Heredity* 68, no. 3 (1977): 3.
80. Ibid, 9.
81. Theodosius Dobzhansky, "Changing Man," *Science* 155 (January 27, 1967): 409.

More recently, the socialist Jeremy Rifkin expressed this concept in picturesque language, as follows:

> Evolution is no longer viewed as a mindless affair, quite the opposite. It is mind enlarging its domain up the chain of species.[82]

> In this way one eventually ends up with the idea of the universe as a mind that oversees, orchestrates, and gives order and structure to all things.[83]

Lest anyone misunderstand, this universal mind is not intended to represent the God of the Bible at all. Harvard University's Nobel prize-winning biologist George Wald, who used to state that he did not even like to use the word *God* in a sentence, has come to realize that the complex organization of the universe cannot be due to chance, and so has become an advocate of this modernized form of pantheism. He says:

> There are two major problems rooted in science, but unassimilable as science, consciousness and cosmology....The universe wants to be known. Did the universe come about to play its role to empty benches?[84]

Modern physicists have played a key role in the recent popularization of evolutionary pantheism, what they have called the "anthropic principle."

> At least the anthropic principle suggests connections between the existence of man and aspects of physics that one might have thought would have little bearing on biology. In its strongest form the principle might reveal that the universe we live in is the only conceivable

---

82. Jeremy Rifkin, *Algeny: A New Word—A New World* (New York: Viking Press, 1983), 188.
83. Ibid, p. 195.
84. George Wald, as reported in Dietrick E. Thomsen, "A Knowing Universe Seeking to be Known," *Science News* 123 (February 19, 1983): 124.

universe in which intelligent life could exist.[85]

This remarkable compatibility of the universe to its human oc-
cupants is not accepted as a testimony to divine design, however,
but as a deterministic outcome of the cosmic mind. The anthropic
principle is emphasized in a quasi-official New Age publication, as
follows:

> Given the facts, our existence seems quite improbable—
> more miraculous, perhaps, than the seven-day wonder
> of Genesis. As physicist Freeman Dyson of the Institute
> for Advanced Study in Princeton, New Jersey, once
> remarked, "The universe in some sense must have
> known we were coming."[86]

Prior to these modern developments, Sir Julian Huxley, arguably
the leading architect of the neo-Darwinian system, had written an
influential book called *Religion without Revelation* and had become,
with John Dewey, a chief founder of the American Humanist Association. As first director-general of UNESCO, he formulated the
principles of what he hoped would soon become the official religion
of the world.

> Thus the general philosophy of UNESCO should, it
> seems, be a scientific world humanism, global in extent
> and evolutionary in background.[87]

> The unifying of traditions into a single common pool
> of experience, awareness and purpose is the necessary
> prerequisite for further major progress in human
> evolution. Accordingly, although political unification
> in some sort of world government will be required for
> the definitive attainment of this state, unification in the
> things of the mind is not only necessary also, but it can

85. George Gale, "The Anthropic Principle," *Scientific American* 245 (December 1981): 154.
86. Judith Hooper, "Perfect Timing," *New Age Journal* 11 (December 1985): 18.
87. Julian Huxley, "A New World Vision," *The Humanist* XXXIX (March/April 1979): 35.

pave the way for other types of unification.[88]

The neo-Darwinian religionists (Huxley, Dobzhansky, Dewey, etc.) thought that evolutionary gradualism would become the basis for the coming world humanistic religion. Evolutionists of the new generation, on the other hand, have increasingly turned to punctuationism—or revolutionary evolutionism—as the favored rationale, largely because the scientific weaknesses in gradualism are increasingly exposed by creationists. This development has facilitated the amalgamation of Western scientism with Eastern mysticism.

> The new systems biology shows that fluctuations are crucial in the dynamics of self-organization. They are the basis of order in the living world: ordered structures arrive from rhythmic patterns....The idea of fluctuations as the basis of order...is one of the major themes in all Taoist texts. The mutual interdependence of all aspects of reality and the nonlinear nature of its interconnections are emphasized throughout Eastern mysticism.[89]

The author quoted, Dr. Fritjof Capra at the University of California (Berkeley), has been one of the New Age movement's main scientific theoreticians, particularly in the application of modern computerized networking and systems analysis to the study of past and future evolution. He also appropriated the unscientific idea of "order through chaos," an ancient pagan notion reintroduced to modern thought, if not to science, by Ilya Prigogine.

The incorporation of Eastern religious evolutionism into Western evolutionary thought was greatly facilitated also by the "Aquarian Age" emphasis of the student revolutions of the sixties. Not all of the scientific New Age followers accept the astrological and occult aspects of the movement, but even these features are becoming more prominent and intellectually acceptable with the growth of the movement's pantheistic dimensions. John Allegro makes the following ominous prediction:

---

88. Ibid. This paper was kept "in-house" by UNESCO for about 30 years before *The Humanist* was allowed to publish it.

89. Fritjof Capra, "The Dance of Life," *Science Digest* 90 (April 1982): 33.

It may be that, despite our rightly prized rationality, religion still offers man his best chance of survival.... If so, it must be a faith that offers something more than a formal assent to highly speculative dogma about the nature of a god and his divine purpose in creation; it must promise its adherents a living relationship that answers man's individual needs within a formal structure of communal worship....Historically, the cult of the Earth Mother, the ancient religion of the witches, has probably come nearest to fulfilling this role, and being sexually oriented has been especially concerned with this most disturbing and potentially disruptive element in man's biological constitution.[90]

Gaia, the religion of the Earth Mother, Mother Nature, is essentially ancient pantheism. It is now returning, even in "Christian" lands, in all its demonic power. When combined with the pervasive controls made possible by modern computerized systems technology, the global goals of evolutionary humanism seem ever imminent indeed. Jeremy Rifkin considers them to be inevitable.

We no longer feel ourselves to be guests in someone else's home and therefore obliged to make our behavior conform with a set of preexisting cosmic rules. It is our creation now. We make the rules. We establish the parameters of reality. We create the world, and because we do, we no longer feel beholden to outside forces. We no longer have to justify our behavior, for we are now the architects of the universe. We are responsible to nothing outside ourselves, for we are the kingdom, the power, and the glory forever and ever.[91]

Those who want to adapt Christianity to our scientific age by compromising with evolution must learn that they are not opening the door to science, but to the Devil's deception from the beginning—the desire to be like God that brought death, disease, disaster,

90. John M. Allegro, "Divine Discontent," *American Atheist* 28 (September 1986): 30.
91. Rifkin, *Algeny*, 244.

and Darwinian decline to a corrupted creation that desperately needs the restoration of new life in Christ. The alternative is the "gospel of death." Rifkin, though certain evolution is the world's future, is despondent. He closes his book with these words of despair:

Our future is secured. The cosmos wails.[92]

New Age evolutionism is not so new, after all; and Mother Nature is really nothing but one of the many faces of ancient Babylon, the "Mother of Harlots,"[93] the age-old religion of God's ancient enemy "which deceiveth the whole world."[94]

Scientifically speaking, New Age evolutionism, with its absurd ideas of order through chaos and quantum speciations, is even less defensible than Darwinian gradualism. Biblically speaking, evolutionism in any form is false, "For in six days the LORD made heaven and earth, the sea, and all that in them is."[95] Instead of a wailing cosmos, "the heavens declare the glory of God; and the firmament sheweth his handiwork."[96] The real "new age" will come when Christ returns!

Evolution in the Last Days

Just as pantheistic evolution served as the world's religion in the early days, so it may again in the last days. The New Age is really nothing but a revival in modern garb of the old age—that is, the first age after the Flood, when King Nimrod led the world in a united rebellion against the Creator.[97] And just as all the groups in the wide spectrum of New Age beliefs are founded upon a base of pantheistic evolutionism, so all have as their ultimate goal, just as Nimrod did, the development of a global system of government, culture, finance, and religion. The United Nations organization has been the focus of these plans, but it will eventually evolve into a much stronger international government in which all

---

92. Ibid, 255.
93. Revelation 17:5.
94. Revelation 12:9.
95. Exodus 20:11.
96. Psalm 19:1.
97. See Genesis 10:8–12; 11:1–9.

the kings of the earth [will] set themselves, and the rulers [will] take counsel together, against the LORD, and against his [Christ], saying, Let us break their bands asunder, and cast away their cords from us.[98]

To accomplish this, they must first teach men once again (as they did in ancient times) to change the "glory of the uncorruptible God into an image made like to corruptible man," and then to "[worship] and [serve] the creature more than the Creator."[99] As Robert Muller, former Assistant Secretary General of the United Nations (presumably speaking on behalf of that organization) once said:

> I believe the most fundamental thing we can do today is to believe in evolution.[100]

Now, if the most fundamental thing that New Age followers (as well as the older style secular humanists and social Darwinists) can do to bring about such a world system is to believe in evolution, that means the most effective thing the remnant of believers in God and His Word can do to offset this is to believe and teach a soundly biblical and scientific creationism. This must include the great truth that the Creator has now also become the Lamb of God, our sin-forgiving Savior, and soon will return as eternal King.

In that day, "These shall make war with the Lamb, and the Lamb shall overcome them: for he is Lord of lords, and King of kings."[101]

THE VITAL IMPORTANCE OF CREATION

It is high time that people in general, and Bible-believing Christians in particular, recognize the foundational significance of special creation. Creation is not merely a religious doctrine of only peripheral importance, as many people (even many evangelical Christians) seem to assume. Rather, it is the basis of all true science, of true Americanism, and of true Christianity. Evolutionism, on the other

---

98. Psalm 2:2, 3.
99. Romans 1:23, 25.
100. Robert Muller, as cited in Kristin Murphy, "United Nations' Robert Muller—A Vision of Global Spirituality," *The Movement Newspaper* (September 1983): 10.
101. Revelation 17:14.

hand, is actually pseudo-science masquerading as science. As such, it has been acclaimed as the scientific foundation of atheism, humanism, communism, fascism, imperialism, racism, laissez-faire capitalism, and a variety of cultic, ethnic and so-called liberal religions, by the respective founders and advocates of these systems. And now it is energizing the fearful New Age religions. The creation/evolution issue is, in a very real sense, the most fundamental issue of all.

Foundation of True Science

Evolutionist presuppositions permeate the writings of modern scientists. Stanley D. Beck says:

> No central scientific concept is more firmly established in our thinking, our methods, and our interpretations, than that of evolution.[102]

But it was not always thus. Beck himself, after defining and discussing the basic premises of science (that is, the existence of a real world, the capability of the human mind to understand the world, the principle of cause-and-effect, and the unified nature of the world) admits that "each of these postulates had its origin in, or was consistent with, Christian theology."[103] That is, since the world was created by a divine Creator and man was created in God's image, therefore nature makes orderly sense, man is able to decipher its operations, and true science becomes possible. If the world is merely the chance product of random forces, on the other hand, then our human brains are meaningless jumbles of matter and electricity, and science becomes nonsense or merely a means of achieving a slight advantage over our closest competitor in Darwin's ceaseless war of nature. Consequently, the great founding fathers of true science (Kepler, Galileo, Pascal, Newton, Boyle, Brewster, Faraday, Linnaeus, Ray, Maxwell, Pasteur, Kelvin, etc.) were almost all creationists and believed they were glorifying God as they proved His works. Yet today such scientists would not even be considered scientists at all, because of their belief in the primeval special creation

---

102. Stanley D. Beck, "Natural Science and Creationist Theology," *Bioscience* 32 (October 1982): 738.
103. Ibid, 739.

of all things by God!

Yet through it all, science has been and still is the Christian's ally in the battle with evolution. Discoveries of science are constantly sending the evolutionists back to the drawing board, while the case for biblical creationism is strengthened with most discoveries. Building science on the Bible continues to lead to one scientific advance after another.

Christians are often criticized for beginning with the Bible, but that foundation has generated a continuing stream of productive scientific hypotheses. Evolutionists want people to believe they begin with the facts. In reality, evolutionists begin with faith in Darwin's words, but the application of that faith leads to constant frustration with the facts. Consider this astonishing admission from the late Stephen Jay Gould, Harvard paleontologist and historian of science and the premier critic of creationism during the last quarter of the twentieth century:

> Phyletic gradualism [gradual evolution] was an *a priori* assertion from the start—it was never "seen" in the rocks.[104]

As discussed earlier, there never has been any fossil evidence of Darwinian evolution. Belief that fossils would show gradual change through transitional forms (missing links) was "an *a priori* assertion from the start," something believed ahead of time. Indeed, how would anyone know proposed evolutionary links were missing unless it was believed ahead of time that they should be found? Basing a scientific prediction on belief is not unscientific, but it is most unscientific to persist in that belief (evolution) when it has been falsified by the facts time and time again.

Since evolution was never based on the fossil evidence (the historical evidence), where did the idea come from? Gould supplies the answer:

> It [gradual evolution] expressed the cultural and political

---

104. Stephen J. Gould and Niles Eldredge, Abstract to "Punctuated Equilibria: The Tempo and Mode of Evolution Reconsidered," *Paleobiology* 3, no. 2 (Spring 1977): 115.

biases of 19th century liberalism.[105]

That is the failed faith that has been forced on our science students for the past century— "the cultural and political biases of 19th century liberalism." Yet for that reason, some Christians have compromised the gospel of Christ.

Since evolution cannot be supported by evidence, it must depend on censorship enforced by lawyers and judges to preserve its privileged position in the public arena. Real scientists fight their intellectual battles in the field and laboratory, looking through telescopes and microscopes; and creation scientists, unlike evolutionists, are willing to let students compare creation/evolution fact for fact, introducing real science, scientific methodology, and the scientific spirit back into the science classroom.

The question is not at all whether faith belongs in the science classroom. Faith is an integral part of science and all other human endeavors. The question is whether only the one favored faith of evolution is allowed, the faith the facts have failed. It is time we restored to the science classroom the openness of testable ideas and the respect for evidence for which the scientific endeavor was once so admired.

Foundation of True Americanism

Although not all of America's great founding fathers were Bible-believing Christians, almost all of them were true creationists, believing that God had created the world and man and all natural systems. The colonies had been settled and developed largely by Christian people who had come to this continent to gain freedom to believe and do what the Bible taught, and they all acknowledged that the foundational belief was belief in special creation. The historian Gilman Ostrander reminds us that

> the American nation had been founded by intellectuals
> who had accepted a worldview that was based upon
> biblical authority as well as Newtonian science. They
> had assumed that God created the earth and all life upon

---

105. Ibid, 115.

it.[106]

Note that these great pioneers were intellectuals, not ignorant emotionalists. They laid great stress on education and science, founding many schools and colleges, in confidence that true learning in any field must be biblically governed. Christian historian Mary-Elaine Swanson says:

> In colonial times, the Bible was the primary tool in the educational process. In fact, according to Columbia University professor Dr. Lawrence A. Cremin, the Bible was the "single most primary source for the intellectual history of colonial America." From their knowledge of the Bible, a highly literate, creative people emerged.[107]

The fact of creation is clearly implied several times in the Declaration of Independence itself in phrases such as *endowed by our Creator, created equal,* and *Nature's God.* Attorney Marshal Foster has pointed out that at least the first twenty-four state constitutions recognized Christianity as the religion of their states.[108] Yet today, the Bible, Christianity, and creationism have been banned from many states and their schools which were founded to teach these very truths! All this has been done through a gross distortion of the First Amendment. The amendment which was intended to prevent the establishment of a particular national denomination (e.g., Catholic, Anglican) has instead been so twisted as to establish evolutionary humanism or even New Age occultism as the quasi-official religion of our public institutions. It is time now to turn attention from the "establishment clause," now so grotesquely misrepresented, to the "prohibition clause": "Congress shall make no law respecting the establishment of religion, nor prohibiting the free exercise thereof."

As intolerant pressure groups have pushed aside belief in the God

---

106. Gilman Ostrander, *The Evolutionary Outlook, 1875-1900* (Clio, MI: Marston Press, 1971), 1.
107. Mary-Elaine Swanson, "Teaching Children the Bible," *Mayflower Institute Journal* 1 (July/August 1983): 5.
108. Marshall Foster, "Christian Offensive of Secular Check-Mate?" *Mayflower Institute Journal* 1 (July/August 1983): 1.

of the Bible in favor of belief in millions of years of struggle and death, American culture has seen the fruits of the Darwinian gospel of death: abortion, euthanasia, racial strife, uncaring competition, and destruction of the family by recreational sex and the promotion of perversion. It is certainly no wonder that evolutionary humanists want to remove all public displays of the cross, nativity scenes, the Ten Commandments, and even our national motto, "In God We Trust." They conveniently forget that their right to be wrong is supported by a public which is still largely Christian!

Foundation of True Religion

True religion must necessarily be based on worship of the world's true Creator. Other religions may deify great men, or man-made systems, or the world itself; but these are all merely variant forms of humanism as men "worship and serve the creature more than the Creator." It is highly significant that all such religions and religious books begin with the creation rather than the Creator, except for the Bible! That is, they all start with the universe already in existence and then try to delineate how the space/time/matter universe somehow developed into its present array of complex systems. This attribute characterizes both ancient paganism and modern humanism; these and all other atheistic, pantheistic, or polytheistic religions are merely various forms of evolutionism. Only in Genesis 1:1 (the foundation of all foundations) is there a statement of the creation of the universe itself. Without this foundation, true religion is impossible.

As a religion, and the basis of numerous man-centered pagan religions, evolution makes statements about the origin, history, and destiny of life and the universe. Unlike true science, which is based on repeatable observations of patterns and processes in the present, evolution is a belief about the past and future, an attempt to reconstruct a unique chronology of events occurring when there are no qualified observers. It assigns unobserved (and unimaginable) creative powers to inanimate matter or to nothing. While it scoffs at the biblical concept of God's creation from nothing (*ex nihilo* or *de novo*), evolutionary humanism emblazons its belief in creation of nothing from nothing on the cover of *Discover* magazine:

46

The universe burst into **something** from absolutely **nothing**—zero, nada. And as it got bigger, it became filled with even more stuff that came from absolutely **nowhere.** How is that possible? Ask Alan Guth. His theory of inflation helps **explain everything.**[109]

At least in the Bible it is not Nothing that created everything; it is the eternally existent, transcendent I AM who created everything from nothing. And the Christian has the record of the acts of God in history, the written Word of the omniscient and omnipotent Creator, as the basis for understanding and framing hypotheses about the true origin, history, and destiny of His creation.

Although creation is the foundation, it is, of course, not the complete structure. Orthodox Jews and Muslims both believe in one eternal Creator, as is revealed in Genesis 1:1, but reject Him as Savior. In addition to the general revelation seen in the creation, God has explicitly revealed Himself through both His Word and His Son. Those who reject either or both cannot know God in His fullness, even though they believe in one God as primeval Creator and, like Christians, are monotheistic. God must be known as gracious Redeemer as well as omnipotent, but offended, Creator. Thus, biblical Christianity is the only complete creationist religion.

Foundation of Christology

By the same token, neither can one know Christ as He really is if one knows Him only as Redeemer. Faint-hearted Christians often justify their lukewarm attitude toward creation by saying that it is more important merely to "preach Christ." They forget that we are preaching "another Jesus"[110] if we do not preach Him as He really is, along with His complete work. The threefold aspect of the person and work of Jesus Christ is beautifully outlined in the majestic declaration of Colossians 1:16–20.

1. Past work, Creation: "by Him were all things created" (v. 16).

2. Present work, Conservation: "by Him all things consist" (v. 17).

---

109. ——. Cover of *Discover* (April 2002).
110. 2 Corinthians 11:4.

3. Future work, Consummation: "by Him to reconcile all things" (v. 20).

The great scope of this threefold work is "all things in heaven and in earth." Jesus Christ was Creator and Sustainer before He demonstrated His love for the unlovely as Savior, in answer to man's sin. The awful price of reconciliation, "the blood of His cross,"[111] is the measure of mankind's terrible offense against our Creator. That offense, furthermore, consists essentially of rejecting His Word, and thus denying that He is really the Creator. One truly preaches Christ only when he first of all presents Him as the Almighty Creator, from whom man was alienated when he repudiated God's veracity in His Word. Only when this is first understood is it really meaningful to speak of God's forgiving grace and saving love, His incarnation and redemptive sacrifice as Son of man. Those who do not believe God created mature man from the dust of the ground have absolutely no reason at all to believe that God could or would raise mankind, with sentient personalities, from the dust of death.

Foundation of Faith

The great message of Christianity is that "the just shall live by faith," speaking of "them that believe to the saving of the soul."[112] But exactly what is this living faith, this saving faith? Faith in the abstract is only naïve sentimentality; the evolutionist's faith in the absence of God is merely self-aggrandizing (and self-destructive) foolishness. To have any substance, saving faith must be faith in something and/or someone.

The faith of which the apostle speaks is outlined in the verses immediately following, in the great faith chapter, Hebrews 11. It is the faith of Abel, offering an acceptable sacrifice; it is Enoch's faith, pleasing God in obedient witness; it is Noah's faith, believing and acting on God's Word; and Abraham's faith, stepping out on God's promises.

But, first of all, it is the foundational faith of Hebrews 11:3, the faith by which "we understand that the worlds were framed by the

---

111. Colossians 1:20.
112. Hebrews 10:38–39.

48

word of God, so that things which are seen were not made of things which do appear." This affirmation clearly tells us that any meaningful faith for salvation and the Christian life must be founded, first of all, on faith in God's special creation of all things, not out of already existing materials but solely by His omnipotent Word!

Foundation of the Gospel

Christ has the might and right to give new and eternal life as Savior because, unlike mortal religious leaders, He is the transcendent author of life as Creator. Many Christians, who either ignore or compromise the biblical doctrine of creation, have urged creationists just to preach the gospel—not creation! But this is impossible, because the saving gospel of the Lord Jesus Christ is squarely founded on creation. The wonderful threefold work of Christ (creation, conservation, consummation) as outlined in Colossians 1:16–20 is identified as "the gospel" in Colossians 1.23. The very last reference to the gospel in the Bible, in Revelation 14:6, calls it "the everlasting gospel" (thus it should never have been any different). This gospel's message is to "worship him that made heaven, and earth, and the sea, and the fountains of waters."[113]

It seems incredible that any Christian would want to compromise the glorious gospel of Christ with "another gospel,"[114] especially the Darwinian gospel of death that assigns (or equates) God's creative power with millions of years of struggle and death. Even ignoring the biblical account of creation in Christian witnessing is dangerous, because it creates a huge stumbling block that prevents many from even considering the good news that struggle and death have been conquered through forgiveness of sin and new life in Christ. Because people have been convinced there is no God by the "vain babblings and oppositions of science falsely so called,"[115] too many (especially students) will not accept the gift of eternal life. Even when they realize just how life-affirming the Christian gospel really is, they are afraid there is no God to keep the gospel's wonderful

---

113. Revelation 14:7.
114. Galatians 1:6.
115. 1 Timothy 6:20.

promises.

While it is surely true that the central focus of the gospel is on the substitutionary atonement and victorious bodily resurrection of Christ,[116] the gospel message also includes His coming kingdom[117] and His great creation. Any other gospel is another gospel and is not the true gospel. Without the creation, the gospel has no foundation; without the promised consummation, it offers no hope; without the cross and the empty tomb, it has no saving power. But when we preach the true gospel with the complete person and work of the Lord Jesus Christ, we build on a sure foundation, can promise a blessed hope, and have available "all power in heaven and earth"[118] through Christ who, in all His fullness, is "with us, even to the end of the world."[119]

116. See 1 Corinthians 15:1–4.
117. See Matthew 4:23.
118. Matthew 28:18.
119. Matthew 28:20.

Appendix

The Compromise Road

There is a disturbing trend among evangelicals today to try to integrate the evolutionary doctrine of naturalistic development with the biblical account of creation. Various hybrid theories have existed for decades, but all of them have emanated from Christians, not evolutionists. As Dr. Henry Morris points out below, this compromise not only does not work, it also seriously undermines the integrity of God's Word.

The basic conflict of the ages is between the two worldviews of evolutionism versus creationism. In its most explicit form, this conflict comes down to biblical revelatory creationism versus evolutionary humanism. The only Book even *claiming* to deal authoritatively with this supernatural creation of the space/time cosmos is the Bible, and there the Creator personally inscribed His explicit summary of creation, as follows: "For in six days the Lord made heaven and earth, the sea, and all that in them is, and rested the seventh day" (Exodus 20:11; see also Exodus 31:15-18).

Evolutionary humanism, on the other hand, purports to explain the origin and development of the cosmos entirely by natural processes innate to the universe itself. In its current form, evolutionism says that the cosmos came into existence as an evolutionary accident, a "quantum fluctuation of some pre-existent state of nothingness." From this remarkable beginning, it evolved through a stage of cosmic inflation, then explosive expansion and eventual formation of elements, stars, planets, animals, and people—all by natural evolutionary processes.

The road of compromise looks attractive at first, but long experience has proved it to be a one-way street. The evolutionists at the end of the road are never satisfied until their opponents travel all the way to the atheistic void at its end.

Charles Darwin set the pattern. Starting out as a Bible-believing creationist, he first became enamored of Charles Lyell's uniformitarianism and his "progressive creationism." Soon he abandoned the Bible and creationism altogether, moving on into the domain of theistic evolutionism. Eventually he became an agnostic and finally an atheist.

Many others in his day followed this compromise road. Darwin's chief opponents, in fact, were scientists, not the theologians of his day. Whole denominations and their religious colleges and seminaries were teaching evolution during Darwin's lifetime, and multitudes of more fundamental Christians were accommodating the evolutionary ages of geology by their "gap theory," "local flood theory," and other devices of artificial biblical exegesis.

But did such compromises ever persuade the evolutionists to meet them half way? The present state of the schools and colleges and the intellectual community in general is the obvious answer.

Despite these lessons of the past, most modern Christians seem oblivious to the fact that all their different accommodational schemes were discredited a hundred years ago and that none of them ever budged the evolutionary establishment from its base of total naturalism.

A good example is found in the writings of Davis Young, who taught geology at Calvin College, an institution belonging to the ostensibly conservative Christian Reformed Church. As a beginning graduate student, Dr. Young originally believed in a literal six-day creation and flood geology. Under the guidance of his Princeton professors, however, he converted to "progressive creationism" and the venerable "day-age theory" of Genesis. This position he strongly advocated in two influential books.[1, 2] He did acknowledge, however, that the "natural" interpretation of Genesis, as well as the teaching of the early Christians and the Protestant reformers, was the literal interpretation. He had simply decided this had to be abandoned because of its supposed geological difficulties. He did, at that time, still hold out for the special creation of a literal Adam and Eve.

His progressive creationism did not even satisfy his theistic-evolutionary colleagues at Calvin, however, let alone his geological peers at the secular universities. So he was now ready to travel further down the road.

I further suggest that both literalism and concordism have outlived their usefulness, and that these approaches should be abandoned for a newer approach that does not try to answer technical scientific questions with Biblical data.[3]

By "literalism," Young means taking the six days of creation as literal days and the flood as worldwide in geological effects, the position advocated by most scientific creationists. By "concordism," he means any theory (gap theory, day-age theory, etc.) that attempts to develop a concordance between the creation record in Genesis 1 and the geological ages. Young now wants to quit trying to relate science and the Bible at all!

I suggest that we will be on the right track if we stop treating Genesis 1 and the flood story as scientific and historic reports.[4]

This approach is essentially that advocated by Christian "liberals" a century ago and now taught in most main-line seminaries.

Another articulate "progressive creationist" is Dr. Pattle Pun, who wrote a book promoting this system. Like Young, however, Pun acknowledged that this is *not* the obvious teaching of God's Word.

It is apparent that the most straightforward understanding of the Genesis record, without regard to all the hermeneutical considerations suggested by science, is that God created heaven and earth in six solar days, that man was created on the sixth day, that death and chaos entered the world after the fall of Adam and Eve, and that all of the fossils were the result of the catastrophic universal deluge which spared only Noah's family and the animals therewith.[5]

The problem with this obvious teaching, according to Pun, is that:

It has denied and belittled the vast amount of scientific evidence amassed to support the theory of natural selection and the antiquity of the earth.[6]

53

The problem with Pun's compromise, however, is that it depends on "all the hermeneutical considerations suggested by science." Did God really need to rely on 20th century scientists to come along one day to tell us what He meant to say? Pun's article, summarizing his book, was published by the American Scientific Affiliation (ASA), the organization of evangelical scientists and theologians which has for decades been leading Christians down this path of compromise with evolution.

To illustrate the lack of appreciation by the secular evolutionists for this service, however, consider the reception accorded ASA's 48-page booklet, *Teaching Science in a Climate of Controversy,* first published in 1986 and distributed free (because of a special grant) to over 60,000 science teachers. The booklet accepts the geological ages and much of evolution, but argues that the process was designed by God, advocating progressive creationism and/or theistic evolutionism as a compromise approach that should satisfy both creationists and evolutionists.

The response of the academic community was almost totally negative. Biologist William Bennetta edited a collection of essays "from leading evolutionists" reviewing the ASA publication, and they all attacked it as viciously as they did the strict creationism of ICR.[7] Stephen Gould, Niles Eldredge, Douglas Futuyma, Michael Ghiselin, and others all contributed bitterly negative critiques to this collection of reviews.

The anti-creationist Committees of Correspondence also came down hard on the booklet,[8] followed by a rather plaintive response by Walter Hearn, one of the booklet's co-authors, complaining that the ASA was merely trying to defend evolutionism against the scientific creationists.[9] Subsequent issues of the C/E Newsletter continued to be filled with attacks on the ASA and its "creationist pseudoscience."

This is ironic. The compromising creationists are attacked as viciously as the strict creationists, by those with whom they are trying to compromise. And in the process, they are rejecting the plain teaching of the Word of God. Even the secular evolutionists can see this.

Many Christians have taken the dishonest way of lengthening the days into millions of years, but the creationists make it clear that such an approach is nothing but a makeshift that is unacceptable Biblically and scientifically....Three cheers, then, for the creationists, for they have cleared the air of all dodges, escapes, and evasions made by Christians who adopt non-literal interpretations of Genesis and who hold that evolution is God's method of creation.[10]

The road of compromise, however attractive it seems, is a one-way street, ending in a precipice and then the awful void of "rational religion," or atheism. Our advice is to stay on the straight and narrow road of the pure Word of God.

References

1. Davis K. Young, *Creation and the Flood* (Grand Rapids: Baker Book House, 1977), 188 pp. See especially pp. 19-25.

2. Davis K. Young, *Christianity and the Age of the Earth* (Grand Rapids: Zondervan Publishing House, 1982), 217 pp. See especially pp. 44-48.

3. Davis K. Young, *Scripture in the Hands of Geologists,* Part I. *Westminster Theological Journal* (Vol. 49, 1987), p. 6.

4. Ibid, Part II, p. 303.

5. Pattle P.T. Pun, "A Theory of Progressive Creationism," *Journal of the American Scientific Affiliation* (Vol. 39, March 1987).

6. Ibid.

7. "Scientists Decry a Slick New Packaging of Creationism," ed. by W. J. Bennetta, *The Science Teacher,* May 1987, pp. 36-43.

8. *Creation-Evolution Newsletter* (Vol. 6, No. 6, 1986), pp. 3-9. Reviews by Robert Schadewald, William Bennetta, and Karl Tezer.

9. *Creation-Evolution Newsletter* (Vol. 7, No. 1, 1987), pp. 16-19.

10. A. J. Mattell, Jr., "Three Cheers for the Creationists," *Free Inquiry* (Vol. 2, Spring 1982), pp. 17-18.

Adapted from Henry M. Morris, "The Compromise Road," *Acts & Facts* 17 (May 1988).

FOR MORE INFORMATION

Sign up for ICR's FREE publications!

Our monthly *Acts & Facts* magazine offers fascinating articles and current information on creation, evolution, and more. Our quarterly *Days of Praise* booklet provides daily devotionals—real biblical "meat"—to strengthen and encourage the Christian witness.

To subscribe, call 800.337.0375 or mail your address information to the address below. Or sign up online at www.icr.org.

Visit ICR.org online

ICR.org offers a wealth of resources and information on scientific creationism and biblical worldview issues.

- ✓ Read our daily news postings on today's hottest science topics
- ✓ Explore the Evidence for Creation
- ✓ Investigate our graduate and professional education programs
- ✓ Dive into our archive of 40 years of scientific articles
- ✓ Listen to current and past radio programs
- ✓ Order creation science materials online
- ✓ And more!

For a free Resource Guide, contact:

INSTITUTE
for CREATION
RESEARCH
P. O. Box 59029
Dallas, TX 75229
800.337.0375